D1466204

# AROUND THE WORLD
# SPAIN

First published in 1997 in the USA by
Thunder Bay Press
5880 Oberlin Drive, Suite 400
San Diego, CA 92121

ISBN 1 57145 081 5

Library of Congress Cataloging-in-Publication Data available upon request

Editions of this book will appear simultaneously
in France, Germany, Great Britain, Italy, Spain
and Holland under the auspices of
Euredition bv, Den Haag, Netherlands

*Translated* from the French by
Tony Burrett and Carla van Splunteren
*Typesetting:* Buro AD, Amersfoort
*Printed* by AUBIN IMPRIMEUR, Poitiers, France

# AROUND THE WORLD
# SPAIN

## Christine Masson

# THUNDER BAY
## P · R · E · S · S

# INTRODUCTION

What image best reflects Spain? That of the matador, standing on tip-toe, every muscle in his body tensed, ready to deliver the fatal thrust? That of a young girl, bra-less under her T-shirt, a broad smile on her face, her books under her arm at the gates of a secondary school? That of an old woman dressed in black and wearing a mantilla, at the door of a church on Sunday morning, surrounded by her loving family? That of dancers in a gay nightclub on Ibiza, wallowing in a metre-thick layer of foam on the dancefloor? That of a king enjoying a family holiday among his subjects at Formentera, taking a dip in the sea as if it were the most ordinary thing in the world? That of an old farmer from La Mancha on the back of a donkey, his silhouette so vividly reminiscent of Sancho Panza? That of the new business woman, alike as two peas in a pod to her modern American counterpart?

Though it is a modern European country, Spain still has an air of mystery, with its tiny white villages where life has remained unchanged since the days of the Catholic Kings; with a city like Barcelona, which offers the very latest in the arts; with a city like Sevilla, on which the eyes of the world were turned at the time of the World Fair (which left the city with nothing but financial problems) and which has now nodded off to sleep again; with its fanatic left-wing movement which has fought for abortion and the legal sale of cannabis; with its places of pilgrimage where crowds of ecstatic worshippers can always be found; with its completely renovated Prado museum, whose collection can compete with the most beautiful (and richest) in Europe. It would not be difficult to list a great many more paradoxes in this land, which once again has become a monarchy and where total democracy holds sway.

Spain contains still more surprises. It is the most touristy country in the world. Every year it is visited by some fifty million holidaymakers, this in a country with a total population of forty million! It lies in the far south-west of Europe and its economic performance since its entry into the EC has surprised many of its partners. It has a young population – only 20% is older than sixty – and during the 'forty year peace' (as the years of Franco's dictatorship are known) a middle class grew up which has increasingly taken over the reins. The result is a balanced and stable country, notwithstanding the fact that it consists of seventeen autonomous regions and despite the problems occasioned by the Basque separatist movement.

For there is something which binds all Spaniards together, from the most aristocratic to the poorest peasant – their country's rich past. Today, Spanish is one of the most widely spoken languages in the world. This is thanks to the fact that 'the sun never set' on the kingdom of Charles V, and to the fact that Philip II's invincible armada managed to make life very difficult for the British navy and so gave the Spanish the opportunity to create a great empire, an empire which still lives on in the memory of a people which provided the world with the greatest conquerors in history. With the passing of the laws concerning divorce in 1981 and abortion in 1985, Spain, Catholic through and through, redefined the role of the Church. After the signing of the new constitution in 1978, in which the division of Church and State was established, the Church quickly signed a number of accords through which the state no longer needed to concern itself with the stewardship of religious pla-

ces. This does not mean, however, that the Spanish have lost their faith: a large number, among them extremely wealthy people, want 0.5% of tax revenue to go to the Church. The days of the Civil War, when priests were thrown of a cliff by the 'reds' with the exhortation that if their God really existed he would give them wings, have long been forgotten. Forgotten, too, is the 'pronunciamiento' of July 18th 1936, the military coup which was the harbinger of the bloody civil war resulting in a thirty-six year dictatorship. Today, it is said more and more that this period was a sort of therapy which put the country in a position to create a healthy society and a healthy economy, essential in a true democracy. The experts who have come to this conclusion also say that the success of the process – set in motion by Franco – which led to a parliamentary monarchy, was largely due to the personality of Juan Carlos.

This 'king who reigns but does not rule' has proved to be a democrat in heart and soul. He is the guardian of the state institutions and during the attempted coup on February 23rd 1981, one word from him was enough to keep his country from chaos. 'Salud, pesetas, y tiempo para gustarlas' (health, wealth, and time to enjoy them), seems to be the motto of the Spanish these days. Children are still brought up with traditional values such as honour, decency and hard work, but nowadays they are told that money can make an excellent contribution to happiness and that they must study hard if they want to earn a reasonable income as adults. On the other hand, the Spanish do not yet appear to be particularly interested in preserving the environment. Air pollution in the big cities, dirty beaches and rivers which are the victims of less than scrupulous industry, are just a few of the negative points. Nonetheless here and there serious ecological movements are coming into being and this growing awareness has resulted in the establishment of a number of national parks. The property developers, who are responsible for the concrete tower blocks which dominate a large part of the Mediterranean coast, must also now take a step backwards as (slowly but surely) legal means of dealing with these scandalous practices are becoming available. The tourist industry is one of the pillars of the economy and the tourists are beginning to be fed up to the back teeth of being caged in concrete. It is therefore no coincidence that the Ministry of Culture has published a brochure in which all the 'white villages' are listed. The idea behind this is that when these villages enjoy more recognition, they will be 'protected' by the tourists. Anyone who now dares to even point a finger at them is now deluged by waves of protest from all over the world.

Young Spanish artists such as the film maker Pedro Almodóvar and the strip cartoonist and designer Mariscal have cast of the mantilla and the matador's suit of lights and are dragging modern youth into the 'movida'. Their Mecca is Barcelona. There can be found a wide range of post-modernist bars and the most diverse galleries where paintings, jewellery and design objects are exhibited a stone's throw away from the works of Gaudí, whose style was completely unorthodox. It should not be forgotten that Spain has produced 'rebels' such as Picasso, Miró and Dalí, who probably invented the word 'unorthodox'!

A penchant for originality is firmly rooted in this people, who attach more value to the word 'pride' than they do to life itself. A well-known tale is that of Eulalia, a thirteen-year-old girl who was tortured by the Romans and then thrown down a well because she had shouted "The old gods are worth nothing and the Emperor is a nobody".

Her soul rose out of the well in the form of a dove and flew straight up to heaven. Of course Eulalia was canonized and up to this day she is venerated in Mérida as the model of faith and independence. Despite this strong independent instinct the Catholic Spanish did not prove to be unduly tolerant with those who did not share their beliefs. The Jews experienced that. As early as the 7th century they were exiled unless they converted, which explains why so many Jews lived in the cities which were under Moorish rule. The Moslems were more tolerant. After the establishment of the Holy Inquisition in 1478, headed by the terrible Torquemada, the position of the Jews was absolutely untenable, even for the 'conversos' (the converted), who were only allowed to stay after the tribunal had established that their conversion was 'genuine and complete'. In 1492, all those Jews who refused to be baptized at the order of the Catholic Kings were thrown out of the country, but even those who did accept baptism were not sure of their lives. Nonetheless, more than three hundred thousand Jews remained in Spain, where they made their contribution to the Golden Age. General Franco rectified matters in the Second World War. He refused to allow German troops – who wanted to attack the British in Gibralter – into his country and thousands of Jews were able to escape to North Africa.

Franco wanted Spain to be 'free, great and one', but the last wish has still not been fully achieved. Only half the population know enough of the Spanish national anthem to sing along, but every Spaniard knows the songs from his own region. In the 16th century, a monarch was 'king of all the Spains', today every Spaniard carries his own 'piece of Spain' in his heart. The Andalusian dreams of bullfights, Moorish edifices, beauties with almond eyes, black hair swirling as they dance with drumming heels. When he is not dreaming of independence, the Basque can always hear the clatter of pelota, the panting of the woodcutters and the sounds of the 'euskera', that strange language which resembles no other whatsoever. The Galician dreams to the drone of the bagpipes and in his dreams sees green valleys where sheep graze, coves with deep inlets where boats pitch heavily in the ocean's breakers. The Catalan regards himself as independent, he angrily defaces road signs not in the Catalan language and defends his autonomy with tooth and nail. The Castilian regards himself as the only true Spaniard. He is proud and tough, sometimes arrogant and knows that the country has him to thank for its unity. And who would not be proud of that?

*Sevilla, at the time of the Feria.*
*Top: young girls in traditional dress,*
*in a caleche.*
*Opposite: a horseman, ready for the*
*parade.*
*Opposite page: top, horsewoman*
*wearing the hat of the masters of the*
*estancias; bottom, flamenco dancers.*

## CHARACTERS OF SEVILLA

A shame perhaps, but the women of Sevilla do not parade around every day in those wonderful dresses with their rustling skirts which suit them so well and seem to have been invented to reflect all their charms. They wear them during the Feria (see pages 59/59) when they play the role of Carmen for every passer-by, a carnation coquettishly placed behind the ear.

The new Constitution of 1978 fundamentally changed the position of the woman and her role in society. The days of blind obedience to her husband and servitude to the men in the family are gone; she no longer has to stand behind the head of the family as he enjoys his meal. But her carefree days are gone too; the right of divorce has put a definitive end to marriage as a 'safe haven' that could never be dissolved. Finally, the free availability of the pill and the right to abortion has definitively freed the woman from masculine domination and the perhaps even greater influence of the Church. Even though most women still marry in white in Spain, it seems that men no longer overly concern themselves with the 'chastity' of young girls. The machos just have to behave themselves! Killing a neighbour to avenge your daughter's honour is a thing of the past and a woman who is unfaithful to her husband is no longer risking her life. But the 'piropo' – a less than sophisticated compliment from a passing man to a woman, particularly in public places (in the street, in a restaurant, at the beach) – is still widely used and seldom taken with offence.

## LA MANCHA

Just as there are regions of commerce and industry, La Mancha is the region of knights and has its very own hero, Don Quixote. He sprang from the imagination of Cervantes, who in his day parodied the extremely popular tales of knights' heroic deeds. As in the story, windmills can still be found in La Mancha (the most beautiful around Consuegra). So, too, can chalk-white houses, hillsides of olive trees so well tended and so carefully planted one behind the other that they appear almost artificial, and vineyards which produce the fresh white wine to which Sancho Panza was certainly not averse. This wine is still always stored in large earthenware jars in a cool, dark place. Admirers of coats of arms can enjoy themselves to their hearts' content in Santa Cruz de Mudela, which was founded for knights on their victorious return from the battle of Navas de Tolosa in the 16th century. Many houses still have beautiful ironwork and bear prestigious coats of arms.

Curiously enough, the inhabitants of La Mancha believe that the Knight of the Doleful Countenance actually existed; some are even seriously trying to discover exactly when and under what circumstances Don Quixote visited their villages! In the beautiful village of El Tobosco a House of Dulcinea has been opened in a 17th century farmhouse and in Belmont one can see the castle where the dauntless knight won his only victory, his defeat of the Knight of the Mirrors.

*Above: the windmills of de la Mancha.*
*Opposite page: An old man with his donkey, an image reminiscent of Sancho Pancha, Don Quixote's companion.*

## ARAGON

This seldom visited region gave Spain its greatest king, Ferdinand, who unified the country by his marriage to Isabella in 1469. Aragon contains part of the Pyrenees, the basin of the river Ebro and the Iberian mountains and therefore does not possess a clear-cut identity of its own. Zaragoza is a city with a rich past which has never completely recovered from the invasions in Napoleonic times. In the cathedral El Pilar stands a miraculous Virgin whose clothes are changed each day. The house in which Goya was born, in Fuendetodos a few kilometres further, is more interesting. Or should we limit our visit to Aragon to the Ordesa National Park which contains various nature reserves and footpaths which flirt with the French frontier? Or would it be better to turn our backs resolutely on the well-trodden paths and proceed to the area around Teruel, the smallest provincial capital in

*Above: the river Cinca.*
*Right: the Quadalquivis.*
*Opposite page: top, the Perdido*
*mountain; bottom, the river Ara.*

of Spain? Though many villages have sadly fallen into decay because of the departure of their inhabitants, there are legends here to be gleaned. The best-known is that of Diego de Marcilla and Isabella de Segura. He was poor and madly in love with her and left to seek his fortune so that her parents, who would have nothing to do with him, could no longer refuse him the hand of their daughter. But she forgot her vow to marry him and wed another on the very day that he returned as a rich man. Diego was so devastated by this that the next day he died of grief. On hearing this Isabella died too, still wearing her wedding dress. Just as tragic is the story of two Moorish architects who were both in love with the same beauty; the rejected lover threw himself from the tower he had built to win the heart of his beloved.

## TAPAS BARS

Spaniards love their wine but in general detest getting drunk, which is why bars always serve snacks – tapas – to accompany a glass. Tapas bars are true institutions of conviviality. Men go there to chat, to meet people and to make appointments in a warm, friendly atmosphere characterized by an extremely high decibel level! A tapa can be almost anything, from a simple cube of jamón serrano (delicious raw ham) to a La Mancha cho) or a half portion (ración), but the most important thing is that during an evening several bars are visited, even if that means standing at the bar when it is very busy. This ritual is so deeply ingrained in daily life that in Madrid, for example, there is a whole circuit that begins at the Puerta del Sol and and ends at the Prado, taking in the calles Espoz y Mina, de la Cruz, Victoria and Núñez Arce on the way. The decor, which usually consists of casks and

*Top: tapas bar.*
*Above: bodega.*
*Opposite page: the bar of the '4 cats' in Barcelona.*

*Following pages: the chapel of Cadaquès.*

cheese croquette (sheep's cheese with a distinctive taste) and might include a salad of garlic potatoes, chipirones (small squid in their own ink), angullas (fried elvers), meat balls in sauce, tripe, large grilled prawns and exquisite cold omelettes. After a while you discover you have eaten a whole meal, rather in the manner of the Lebanese with their mezze. According to your appetite you can order a large portion (pin-

old posters, is very important and the oldest bars, such as Los Gabrieles (on the calle Echegaray), are proud of their 'azulejos'.

## THE CHAPEL OF CADAQUÉS

Contrary to what one might think, more than just the railway station in Perpignon existed for Dali. Cadaqués and its ravishing little white chapel also played a large role in his life. The Saint-Tropez of the Costa Brava, which was chosen as a holiday resort by a small group of painters, deserves more than this nickname, if only because it has managed to resist the overtures of the property developers who have filled much of the surrounding area with concrete tower blocks. Cadaqués is protected by its position; it is surrounded by mountains, hidden at the bend of a cove and, moreover, it has hardly any beach. It is therefore not so surprising that Dali chose Port Lligat for his country house with its bizarre statues on the roof. Sadly one cannot enjoy the crazy interior because the house is a sort of stronghold and is not open to visitors. But admirers of the great master can visit the Moore museum and see his tubes of paint, his letters, and drawings and sketches for new works. True lovers of Dali's work must visit Figueras, where Dali himself founded his own museum in the old municipal theatre. The result is crazy and shows the most important periods in the artist's life through astonishing works as the Venus with Drawers, the liquid watches, the robot in its plexiglas coffin and a wonderful series of portraits of Gala and the painter himself. Three floors of fantasy and delirium that carry the visitor away from the white-plastered facades of the respectable churches of Catalan.

## GUADALUPE

The little wooden statue of the Black Madonna, which was discovered in the 12th century by a shepherd and said to have been carved by Saint Laurent, has played an important role in the history of Spain. Miraculous powers have been ascribed to it and it quickly became the object of pilgrimages and processions. Its fame soon spread beyond the frontiers of Extremadura. After one of his victories over the Moors Alfonso XI had a sumptuous monestary built there. It was dedicated to the Virgin Mary and used by the order of Hieronymites. It is not surprising that Christopher Columbus named one of his discoveries, the island of Guadeloupe, after this image as a mark of honour to 'the patron saint of all the Spains'. Nor was it simply coincidence that he chose to have the Indians he brought back from his voyages baptized in the fountain of Guadelupe. One third of the men who sailed with him on his voyages of discovery came from Extremadura.

The Madonna quickly made the city rich. It became a sort of cross between Lourdes and Rome and in the 15th century could pride itself on its various hospitals, huge herds of livestock and a university of medicine and surgery, the likes of which was unknown in Europe (Pope Nicholas V had given the monks dispensation to dissect bodies). The city was a flourishing centre for four centuries, but in 1809 it was plundered and twenty years later the monks left. Today, the tourists who come to admire her treasures – the Madonna, naturally, but also the eight wonderful paintings by Zurbarán in the sacristy – are guided round by Franciscans.

*Above: the monastery of Guadeloupe.*
*Opposite page: top, the ambulatory of*
*the cloister; bottom, (black) wooden*
*statue of the Virgin Maria.*

*Top: the Palais Royal.*
*Above right: the Royal Guard*
*parades.*
*Opposite page: top, plaza Mayor;*
*bottom, agricultural landscape in the*
*Sierra de la Candeleria.*

## MADRID

A modest provincial town until Philip II decided to move his court there and declared it his capital city, Madrid adapted quite naturally to its royal destiny. Although the courtiers had to be dragged there kicking and screaming, the clergy and the nobility hastened there en masse. A large area of forest had to be cut down to make way for the rapidly-expanding city and this resulted in its well-known dry climate. Madrilenos were content with badly maintained housing and churches. It was only under Philip V, who had the present-day royal palace built, that the city acquired a little more allure. The kings who followed him all made their contributions – Charles III the Prado; Ferdinand VI the Royal Academy and in the 15th century the Buren Retiro park was laid out in the dusty city so that the courtiers could breathe a little fresh air. After it had been neglected for years, Philip VII restored its royal allure and opened it to the general public.

Today, the Royal Guard on parade is a sight worth seeing. The king himself actually lives very simply in the Palacio de la Zarzuela, a few kilometres outside Madrid. The Spanish court is the least expensive in Europe and the king has a personal staff of only seven. Nonetheless he carries out fully the duties laid down for him in the Constitution – safeguarding the proper functioning of state institutions and acting as commander of the armed forces. He discharged these functions royally during the attempted coup of February 23rd 1981 when he appealed to his officers to remain loyal to the government.

*Above: the statue of Philip III, plaza Mayor.*
*Opposite page: plaza de Cibeles with its popular goddess in her chariot drawn by lions.*

## MADRID

Immediately after he had been crowned king of Spain Joseph I, the brother of Napoleon, who was used to the boulevards of Paris, drew up a scheme to spruce up Madrid (gardens were laid out, trees planted along the broad avenues, and so on). This plan did not meet with the full approval of the Madrilenos, who gave him the derisive title of 'Rey Plazuelas' – the King of the Squares'. It is strange that this plan encountered such opposition because the Spanish attach great importance to their squares. The 'paseo' plays an important role in everyday life. Without it there would be no ritual of the evening stroll when people see others and allow themselves to be seen, when they greet each other and stop for a chat, when they take a glass or two. Just like Madrid, the smallest village has its own Plaza Mayor, impressive or simple, but always of essential importance. In big cities like the capital, which today has three million inhabitants, every district has its own squares. Whether they are large or small, monumental or simply of beaten earth, every one of them has the same irreplaceable function. The largest squares, where broad avenues end and which pedestrians can only cross through underground subways, are found in the eastern part of Madrid. Although this monumental style might seem a little excessive – particularly the Plaza de la Cibeles, which contains a statue of a goddess in a chariot drawn by lions, the Head Office of the Banco de España, the Head Post Office and the Ministry of Defence – nonetheless, at the first breath of spring the pavement cafés appear everywhere.

*Opposite page: statue of Velasquez in the Prado.*

Although one of Spain's loveliest monuments, El Escorial, lies 35 kilometres outside the capital (see Toledo, pages 31), Madrid itself also has a great deal to offer – and not only great edifices such as the Prado Museum, which houses one of the richest collections in Europe. Velazquez guards the entrance, but not only Spanish master works can be found in this 18th century building. It was originally built to house the royal collections and was officially brought into use as a museum in 1819 by Ferdinand VII, after a plan by Joseph 1 (Bonaparte). It is impossible to list all the three thousand works, which even after the recent restoration cannot all be exhibited at the same time! Of course Spanish painters such as Goya, Velázquez and El Greco are the best represented, with the Meninas from the court of Philip IV, the Capitulation of Breda, the 'black' Goyas, the portraits of the royal family and the fascinating 'Maya desnuda', but there are countless religious tableaux. Murillo's and Zurbarán's images of Saint Hieronymus cannot be counted. The remainder of the collection is also marvellous, with beautiful works by Rubens, Breughel the Elder and the Younger, Hieronymus Bosch, a magnificent Annunciation by Fra Angelico, Botticellis, Raphaels and several Durers, to mention only the most important works. The Prado must not be missed though a single visit is insufficient to see everything this rich collection has to offer.

*Top: the Prado museum.*
*Above: the Escurial.*

## ARANJUEZ

The Spanish kings, with the building of the Casa del Labrador (literally 'farmer's house), arrived later than others at the idea of imitating rural life. The Casa del Labrador, after the example of the Petit Trianon in Versailles, was only begun in 1803 under Charles IV. It is happy mixture of 18th and 19th century styles and is crammed with rare types of marble, expensive hardwoods and red velvets. But the most beautiful things are the murals on which the greatest painters of the day worked, the most important of them being Zacaría González Velásquez. There are interesting curiosities such as ingenious clocks, inlaid furniture and the sumptuous carved door of the king's toilet. A guided tour only lasts half an hour, but an entire day can be spent in the princely gardens (Jardín de Príncipe) which are full of Boutelou's 18th century statues. One can wander from fountain to lake, from pavilion to island (there are three, linked by a lovely little white marble bridge), in the company of the Madrilenos who en masse take the wonderful steam train (named the 'strawberry train') which from mid-May to mid-October on Saturday and Sunday makes the hour-long journey from Madrid to Aranjuez. Right at the end lies the Casa de Marinos, a pavilion built by Charles III. It contains wonderful royal pleasure craft, including that of Philip IV (a gift from a rich Venetian), that of Charles IV (decorated by Maella) and those of Isabella II, Alfonso XII and Alfonso XIII.

## ARANJUEZ

Aranjuez lies about 50 kilometres from Madrid and its gardens, which are irrigated by the river Tagus and produce delicious asparagus and succulent strawberries, form a sort of oasis in the arid Castilian landscape. In the 18th century the Bourbons chose this peaceful little city as their summer residence and it contains enormous royal edifices which bear no relationship to its unpretentious status. The Royal Palace, which was begun under Philip II and intended to be a second Versailles, is rather disappointing, despite the throne room in passionate rococo style, the porcelain room in Chinese style and the Arabic room which is reminiscent of the Alhambra in Grenada. Actually it is the gardens which are of the most interest. One of these, the Jardín de Parterre – which was also designed by Boutelou – has a Hercules fountain which, with its two pillars, depicts the Straits of Gibralter.

To visit the Jardín de la Isla, designed by Herrera in the 17th century, one must cross a tributary of the Tagus. These gardens also contain monumental fountains and exude a peace which attracts many Madrilenos. Strangely enough, most tourists give Aranjuez a miss. Yet it is a delightful little city with a Baroque church dedicated to San Antonio de Bonavía; a monastery, built by Sabatini, which houses a number of beautiful paintings and, in particular, the Baroque Oficios and Caballeros houses and a number of classical palaces. One more thing – it is well worthwhile visiting La Rana Verde (a very popular little restaurant in the square in front of the palace) to taste the locally-grown asparagus and strawberries.

*Previous page: the house of the ploughman at Aranjuez.*

*Opposite page: the park of Buen Retiro in Madrid.*
*This page: top, the garden of the Palais Royal in Aranjuez; bottom, the church of San Antonio de Bonavia in Aranjuez.*

*Above: view of the city of Toledo.*

*Opposite page: the cathedral of*

*Toledo.*

## TOLEDO

Anyone who has seen the savage sky above Toledo, the mare's tail clouds at sunset, the dark grey tints of a stormy evening knows the source of inspiration of El Greco – or Domenikos Theotokopoulos. The Santa Cruz museum has some twenty of his works on exhibition. El Greco, one of the greatest painters of the 17th century, was thrown out of the royal residence of El Escorial by Philip II, which does not say a lot for the king's discernment in matters of art. In the past Toledo was under West Gothic, then Islamatic and finally Catholic rule, but from the 11th to the 13th century it was also the capital of the Spanish Jews. The cathedral with its Gothic, Moorish, Baroque and Neo-Classical influences is a witness to this richly-hued past. The Alcázar, dominating the skyline of the city, was built in the 16th century for the the first governor...El Cid.

El Escorial, a palace-monastery built in austere architectural style, is in the form of the grill on which St. Laurentius, venerated by Philip II, died a martyr's death and it does not easily yield its secrets. It was constructed of grey granite under the supervision of successively Juan Bautista, a pupil of Michelangelo, and Juan de Herrera. The room of Philip II is so constructed that it offers a direct view of the high altar of the chapel, but the successors of the monk-king made many changes. For example, the apartments of the Bourbons, furnished by Philip V, with their tapestries, marble floors and gilded marble clocks, give the palace a more royal allure.

## BURGOS

In the course of the centuries Burgos was at various times the capital of Spain, but the city is particularly known for its extraordinary cathedral which, according to Philip II, was the 'work of angels'. The construction of the stone lacework which makes the cathedral one of the high points of the Gothic style took three hundred years to complete. There is so much to see that it takes a visitor at least an hour to form a changed sides as often as he changed his shirt – he sometimes fought alongside the Arabs, sometimes against them (he took Valencia from them) – the legend is the important thing. The marriage certificate of the famous lovers can be seen in the cloister. Here, too, is the chest pledged to a usurer in return for money, on condition that he should only look to see what treasure it contained after a year had passed. According to legend, the usurer never

*Above: the cloister of the cathedral.*
*Right: the monastery de las Hueglas.*
*Below: the chapel of Connetable.*
*Opposite page: the church of the*
*monastery de las Hueglas.*

decent impression of all this beauty (there are some twenty lovely little chapels) and of all the curios such as the papamoscas (a standing clock with automatic movement), the image of Christ made of buffalo skin and human hair with its wierd human expression, the tree of Jesse, the solid silver image of the Virgin Mary on the high altar and many more beautiful or unusual things such as the grave of El Cid and Jimena. Without a shadow of doubt El Cid was the most famous inhabitant of Burgos. It is of no concern that he saw through the ruse because El Cid was able to pay him back in time. Another legend, certainly based on fact, tells that El Cid wished to be buried together with his wife, his children and his horse Babicca, in the monastery of San Pedro de Cardena. In 1921, their remains were brought to the cathedral. In 1940, out of curiosity, the Duke of Alba had excavations carried out in the former grave. These revealed the skeleton of a horse.

## AVILA

Avila should preferably be visited in the winter, when the wind dusts the surrounding hills with a thin layer of snow and the city seems to retreat behind its great ramparts. These were built in the 11th century on the orders of Alfonso VI after he had captured the city from the Moors and are 12 metres high, 3 metres thick, more than 2 kilometres in length and contain 9 fortified gates. Protected by its walls, this unusual city has been able to resist all political and even tourist overtures, doubtlessly drawing strength from 'its' saint, Teresa of Avila, who was elevated to Doctor of the Church by the Pope in 1982 (though she died in 1582). After the inevitable stroll round the city and a visit to the cathedral built into the walls, it is well worth visiting the convent – out of religious interest or not – which is built on the site of the house in which she was born and which bears her name, the museum with its few relics and, in particular, the Encarnación convent where she made her vows and where she lived some forty years. Besides her cell, visitors can also see the little room where she received her confessor, San Juan de la Cruz, who was obsessed with the same penchant for the mystical as she. It is also interesting that according to some sources this saint from a noble family was of Jewish descent and that her parents only allowed her to enter the convent in order to hoodwink the terrible Inquisition.

## SALAMANCA

They are young, bearded and dressed like their ancestors – black velvet trousers and doublet, lace-trimmed shirt and white stockings – sing old ballads accompanying themselves on the guitar and from the first sunny days on can be found in pavement cafés and restaurants throughout southern Europe. They are ordinary students from Salamanca who finance their holiday or their journey in this way. It is a tradition that was created when Alfonso IX of León, in an attempt to compete with his cousin Alfonso VIII of Castile, founded a university in Salamanca to rival that in Plasencia. His plan succeeded beyond his expectations because in the 14th century Salamanca was on the same level as the Sorbonne and two hundred years later seventy different subjects were taught to some 12,000 students. Men such as Cervantes and Cortéz wore out their trousers on the benches of this university.

Students no longer spend the night before an exam in the chapel of St. Barbara, their feet on the grave of a bishop to bring them luck, nor do they write their names in bull's blood when they have graduated. But they are still an important part of the beautiful Plaza Mayor, where under the 18th century arcades the pavement cafés are thronged with the youngsters.

*Left page: top, decorated ceiling of the patio de las Escuelas; bottom, inscription on the wall of the patio. Above: sculpted fronton at de las Escuelas.*

## SALAMANCA

Returning to the university after being imprisoned for four years by the Inquisition, Fray Luis de León, one of the greatest teachers of the Golden Age, began his lecture with the words "As I said to you yesterday..." These words could well apply to the Salamanca of today. The ancient university buildings, a high point of Plateresque style, are still in use. On the way to the Patio de las Escuelas one still passes the wonder-

and which is decorated with the star constellations and the signs of the zodiac. Perhaps Christopher Columbus saw this room when he came to ask the astonomers' advice before he set sail.

The whole city is full of coats of arms and stone ornaments which are evidence of a rich past, a past that sometimes still seems close – the group of gargoyles, for example, which the terrible Bishop Fonseca had made in the likeness of his

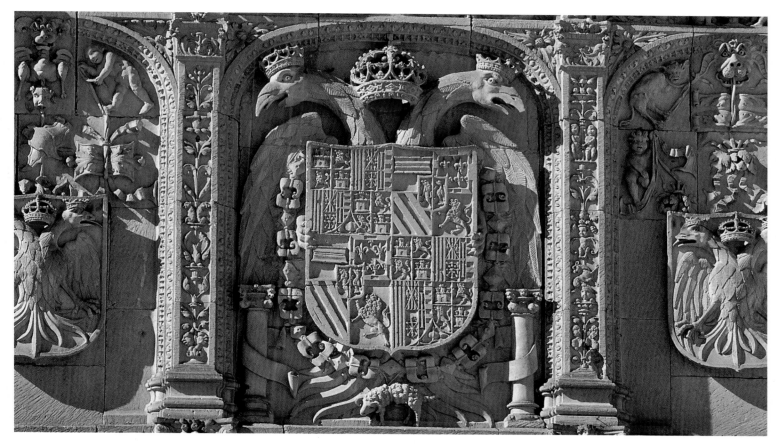

ful facade with its medal portraits of the Catholic Kings and its breathtakingly apt, even allogorical, figures. On the first floor they bow their diligent heads over the collection of some 160,000 ancient books. Students have always studied hard beneath the ceilings with the caissons and under that of one of the halls of the Escuelas Menores, where in days gone by astrology (then an exact science) was taught,

enemies, to adorn his house, the Casa de Salina. A durable form of humour!

*Opposite page: stone escutcheons.*
*Top: church tower of Clerecia.*
*Above: escutcheon detail.*
*Below: the house of the Conchas.*

39

*Above: the Santiago de Caballero church.*
*Right: its partly orange-coloured dome.*
*Opposite page: a view of the old city.*

## ZAMORA

This peaceful city on the banks of the Douro, named 'the very noble and loyal city' by Henry IV, was the backcloth to a fierce battle between Moors and Christians. The city proved not to be so loyal after all, because King Sancho II was murdered there. A gate was built – the traitors gate – so that this base deed would never be forgotten.

The Casa del Cid, and the church of Santiago de Caballeros where he was knighted, are in themselves not worth making the journey to Zamora for but the cathedral, which has a tower which would not be out of place in Byzantium, is extremely interesting. The sight of the enormous dome, which looks like an orange cut into segments, is well worth a stiff neck! And those who love symbolism should not miss the sculpted 15th-century rooms.

As in many Spanish cities, processions and celebrations take place here in Holy Week. Zamora has four processions; a silent procession, the procession of las Capas, that of the Miserere Gisant and finally that of the Cinco de Copas. But the largest number of participants (some 3,000) take part in the procession which leaves before sunrise on Good Friday, though the habits, perhaps, do not deserve to be imitated. It is said that the penitents hide bottles of wine under their clothing in order to give them courage and allay the rigours of the march. When the throng arrives, towards twelve noon, some are so much the worse for wear that perhaps it should be known as the 'procesión de los borrachos' (the drunks' procession).

## SEGOVIA

Under the Romans Segovia was a military fort and the city is a curious mixture of martial architecture, history (Segovia is where Isabella was crowned queen of Castile and where the terrible Grand Inquisitor, Torquemada, had his headquarters) and legends. The best-known legend is probably that of the Roman aqueduct; it was said to be the work of the devil who for once fell into his own trap. A young girl, who had to fetch water before she was allowed to dance, made a pact with the devil. In exchange for her soul he would fetch water for her before it was day, so that she could go to the ball. The girl left and the devil immediately began work on the viaduct which had to be ready before the morning. But the girl was so sorry for what she had done that she did not go to the ball

*Top: the San Ildefonso palace.*
*Above: the castle of Coca.*
*Opposite page: top, the cathedral of*
*Segovia; bottom, the Alcazar.*

but began to pray instead. God heard her prayers and ensured that the devil did not finish his work in time. At the place of the last stone is an effigy of the Virgin Mary.

The Alcázar, which dominates the skyline of the city, is like a fairytale castle (it dates from the 14th century).

There is also a tale attached to the palace of San Ildefonso. It was built by Philip V, the grandson of Louis XIV, who missed Versailles so much that he had a replica built.

Just a few kilometres further lies the castle of Coca. Its pure Moorish style makes it a must for postcard collectors. Its 'legend' is a simple one – it is one of the most beautiful castles in Spain.

## TRUJILLO

Trujillo, with its clock towers in which storks nest, actually seems more like a large village when one sees it for the first time. It is difficult to believe that Francisco Pizarro, one of the most remarkable explorers from the times of the Great Discoveries, was born here. Trujillo owes its rich architecture – in particular the palace of the Marqués de la Conquista, built by Hernando Pizarro, brother of Francisco and companion on his voyages – to the gold of the Incas.

Francisco was the illegitimate son of an aristocrat and, like most youngest sons of the aristocracy, received an excellent education. Nonetheless, like his brothers he had no hope of a position in Spanish society which would satisfy his ambitions. He therefore left for the New World, together with his brothers and his best friend, Almagro, who many years later would murder him in Lima. Together with a handful of men who had a complete disregard for their own safety, Pizarro forced a way across the continent and finally reached Peru, then the kingdom of the Incas. Because of his courageous exploits, Charles V gave him the funds and ships necessary to carry out his plan of conquest. The death of emperor Atahuelpa crowned his victory.

Today, youngsters climb impudently up the statue of the local hero which dominates the square and in the shadow of the charming Moorish Torre del Alfiler Trujillo dreams peacefully about its days of glory.

*Opposite page: Torre del Alfiler,
where the swallows nestle.
Above: castle of Trujillo.*

*Following pages: a chapel in the
countryside near Trujillo.*

## CACERES

It is not by chance that the centre of Cáceres is named the 'barrio monumental'. After the Reconquista, aristocratic families from various provinces moved here and spent most of their time (at any rate until the end of the 15th century) trying to outdo each other in the building of palaces. The city is a paradise of heraldic architecture, a sort of open-air museum of Spanish Gothic. It is ringed by a defensive wall inherited from the Moors and lies in the centre of a landscape of arid plateaus where herds of sheep wander.

Nothing appears to disturb the peace of Cáceres and as evening falls it is strangely still in the tiny winding streets, here and there interrupted by a few steps, between the palaces. It almost seems as if the town is trying to forget the tumult and enthusiasm of days gone by. For it was here in Cáceres, on October 29th 1936, that Franco was proclaimed head of state,

*Above: barrage of Alcantara.*
*Right: plateau of los Castanas.*
*Opposite page: top, the ramparts of*
*Caceres; the landscape at la Huerta.*

in a house which in the 12th century sheltered a group of intrepid French knights who had come at the request of the king to settle accounts with the Moors. The 'Golfines', however, proved to be so aggressive, so the story goes, that even the king could not control them. Another house, that of the Toledo-Moctezuma family, proves that the conquistadors, inspired as they were by the highest Christian intentions, were also ordinary men. This house was built at the commission of Juano Caro Moctezuma, son of a daughter of the Aztec king Moctezuma and sired by a Spaniard.

## SEVILLA

Now that the World Fair of 1992 has been held on its soil, Sevilla can rightly call itself the capital of Andulusia. In its long existence the city has known glorious times and times when it was little more than an insignificant provincial town. Sevilla's history began with the Romans, who made it the capital of Batica (after it had been captured by no less a personage than Caesar). After the invasion of the Vandals, first voyage round the world and Christopher Columbus is buried in its cathedral. In 1649 the city was struck by an epidemic which wiped out half its population. Economic disasters, political incidents and finally the French occupation ensured that its prestige slowly but surely declined. In the Civil War, the city again acquired a prominent role; it was one of the nationalists' bases. Defeat was a bitter blow to the city and it was only when tourists began

*Above: tile decorations at the Plaza de España.*
*Right: the garden of the Alcazar.*
*Below: the Pilatos house.*
*Opposite page: the gardens of the Alcazar.*
*Following pages: the Guadalquivir.*

however, the city returned to anonymity. In 712, the Moors made it the rival of Cordoba. Various Arab occupiers gave the city palaces and monuments, among which was the famous Giralda (an old minaret integrated in the huge cathedral built between 1402 and 1506) and the delightful Patio de los Naranjos, which today is all that remains of what was once a great mosque. In 1248 the city was recaptured by the Christian kings and soon adapted to the spirit of the period of the great conquests. In 1519 Magellan left Sevilla on his to flock to the city and the region began to develop that Sevilla recovered its famous 'alegría'.

*Above: impressive arches at Santa Cruz.*
*Opposite page: left, a patio at Santa Cruz; right, the palace of Alcazar.*

*Following page: la Plaza de España in Sevilla.*

54

## SEVILLA

The architecture of Sevilla owes much to its Arab occupiers. Patios, arabesques, arcades and fountains were directly inherited from them, not to mention the monuments built during the caliphate. These include the magnificent, purely Moorish 14th-century Alcázar, which is particularly famous for its colourful azulejos and its park with lakes and palm trees, and the Torre del Oro, a mysterious fortified structure that towers above the river. Sevilla also has a Jewish quarter, the barrio de Santa Cruz, which is a big network of little streets and white houses with baroque balconies and inner courtyards full of flowers. This shows a completely different face of the city, which is tolerant enough to have a gypsy quarter. This is the barrio de Triana on the other side of the Gua-

dalquivir. Popular yet without great charm, according to tradition it was here that the flamenco was born.

The semi-circular Plaza de España is constructed as an ode to the provinces. It has an allegorical mosaic for each of them which can be admired under what nowadays is the benevolent watching eye of the huge headquarters of the army and of local government. But Sevilla is also Spanish and Catholic. The huge cathedral is witness to this (116 metres long, 75 metres wide and 56 metres high inside). Its riches include a glittering golden reredos and a cross made from the first cargo of gold ore that Christopher Columbus brought back with him.

*Top: a flamenco dancer.*
*Above: Feria parade.*
*Opposite page: top, Sevillan women*
*and their horsemen; bottom,*
*Carmen relives.*

## THE FERIA OF SEVILLA

In Sevilla the people live from one great religious festival to the next. Corpus Christi (the Day of Sacraments) on December 8th is particularly important, but the festival of the year is the Feria (traditionally held between the 18th and 23rd of April – at least if this coincides with Easter).

There is so much to do! Bullfights, huge costumed processions, extremely chic receptions – for days the entire city lives once more in the days of Carmen. The Sevillian women wear zany dresses with rustling flounces, the men once again become bold knights and the prado San Isidro is transformed into a village of 'casetas', shaky booths of wood and canvas in which private parties are held. The best-known families invite their friends and the big companies fête their most important customers. Eating, drinking, dancing the flamenco, goes on day and night in an exuberant party atmosphere, less than a hundred metres from the cigarette factory of... yes, of Carmen! During the Feria all Spanish women have the fiery glance of the renowned gypsy, whether they are parading past in a coach, sumptiously dressed; riding into the city behind their escort, dresses draped over their horse's croup or even in the saddle, soberly dressed and wearing the same black hat worn by the masters of the great estancias. On the last evening there is a gigantic firework display, but the hardiest dance on until the first light of dawn.

## RELIGIOUS FESTIVALS AND PILGRIMAGES

Although since the new Constitution of 1978 Catholicism is no longer the state religion, it still has an important place in everyday Spanish life. Countless processions and festivals are still organized by the numerous brotherhoods (Sevilla has more than fifty).

Every church has its own treasure, usually a beautifully decorated image of Christ or the Virgin Mary, which is paraded through the streets of the city on huge floats drawn by penitents. When the procession comes to a halt, prayers are said. The strangest procession is probably that known as the 'procession of the Nazarene' in Puebla del Carminal in La Coruña which has taken place since the 15th century. Families walk in procession behind a statue of Christ, carrying an empty coffin which either symbolizes their prayers for a member of the family who is sick or simply their gratitude for restoration of health. In other cities a prisoner is released in the name of Our Lord, he walks in front of the procession with a cap on his head.

Such processions might be religious through and through, but they are not dull or sanctimonious. Passers-by often stop to watch the parading penitents and to listen to the heartrending canticles (the famous saetas). But that does not stop them from eating and drinking at the tables which are always set up in the neighbouring streets, festooned with Chinese lanterns. And the solemnities may well be followed by a corrida, as they are in Holy Week.

*Opposite page and top this page: penitents in a procession. Above: procession during the 'semana santa'.*

## CORDOBA

The only Arabic legacy Cordoba still has is its architecture – but what architecture! True, the great library has gone up in flames and not much remains of the three hundred mosques and countless palaces built by the Moors under Abd El Rahman III (who was caliph in 929) and his successor Al Hakam – although what does remain is splendid. But in the drowsy streets there is always a hint of distant cultures, an almost imperceptible elegance emphasized by masterworks of rare beauty.

One searches in vain for a trace of the philosopher and mathematician Averroes or the famous Jewish scholar Maimonides – not to mention Seneca, the tutor of Nero. This provincial city has forgotten everything for which it was once so famed, though the memory of it still clings to the stones of its most important monuments. First and foremost, of course, is the cathedral. The eight hundred and fifty pillars of the splendid mosque are now the pillars on which the presbytery rests and the mihrab, a jewel in marble, was miraculously spared by the Christians who (for once) showed tolerance, perhaps because they had never seen anything quite so elegant. As Théophile Gautier remarked "Córdoba is more African than any other city in Andalusia (...) Should the Moors return they would need to change little to feel at home again." And he was right. From the Patio de los Naranjos and the Zoco (a sort of souk) to the tiny streets with their pens and little white houses leaning against each other, between them here and there a palm tree, – everything is strongly reminiscent of Morocco.

*Opposite page: doors of the mosque
which became a sanctuary for
Christians.
This page: top, the mosque's hall with
850 marble columns; below, detail of
the facade of the mosque.*

## GRANADA

This city, which owes everything to its Arab occupiers – its affluence (the Moors introduced the irrigation system which makes the plain around the city so fertile), its fame (the Alhambra and its gardens attract visitors from all over the world) and even its name – has a most enthralling history. Until 1492, Granada was under Islamitic rule and has a tragic love story to thank for its 'liberation' by the Catholic Kings. Mulay Hassan, without no problems whatsoever, he was able to demand the city from his vassal, who was forced into exile. On January 2nd 1492, the Castilians took back Granada after five centuries of Moorish rule.

This event is remembered at a place which bears the name 'Suspiro del Moro' (literally the Moor's Sigh); a hill where Boabdil turned to catch his last glimpse of the city. His mother, the temperamental Aïcha, upbraided him for his weakness with

*Previous pages: view of the Albacin quarter of Granada.*
*This page: top, the gardens of Generalife; above, the gardens of the Alhambra.*
*Opposite page: the Abbey of Sacro Monte.*

ruler of this wonderful 'emirate' was stupid enough to fall in love with a Christian, the beautiful Zoraya, and for her he abandoned his lawful wife Aïcha, mother of his son (and future successor) Boabdil. War broke out and Mulay Hassan was defeated. Ferdinand of Aragon sized his opportunity; taking the far-too-young king Boabdil prisoner and forcing him to swear an oath of allegiance before freeing him. A few months later, the angry words: "Weep like a woman for what you could not defend as a man."

*Above and right: the courtyard with lions at the Alhambra.*
*Opposite page: patio at Mechouar.*

## GRANADA

After they had captured Granada the
Catholic monarchs Ferdinand and
Isabella, despite being deeply Christian, did not destroy the great edifice
of their predecessors. The Alhambra
– "to which benevolent spirits have
given the lustre of a dream and filled
with harmony," as Victor Hugo
wrote – was even restored by Ferdinand and Isabella and served as ac-
commodation on their journeys. The
Alcázar would not be out of place in
the tales of the thousand and one
nights. It has a rare beauty, whether
it is viewed from the lovely Salón de
Embajadores with azulejos bearing
texts from the Koran, the entire city
at your feet, or whether the unique
cupola is seen from the Sala de las
Dos Hermanas, which has more than
five thousand small honeycomb-like
holes. But even more than to the

royal residences built by the Sultans,
Granada owes its fame to its beautiful gardens and fountains. The Alhambra is a poem in stone but also an
ode to the taming of nature. Water
murmers along its lanes, sometimes
spouting high into the air in captiva-
ting song and then flows chuckling
on. Every hour of the day and night
the gardens of the Generalife, full of
the scents and the sounds of water,
play an ancient game of seduction
which no-one can resist. Nor can one
evade the charm of the ancient flamenco rhythms of the gypsies, who
have settled on the Sacromonte, a
hill opposite the Generalife. Here
there are caves in which not alto-
gether authentic, alas, dancing and
drinking rooms have been established.

*Top: at Domecq, a sherry producer.*
*Above: grape harvesting.*
*Opposite page: top left, the Domecq*
*bodega; top right, a taster; below,*
*vineyards.*

## JEREZ

According to legend the 15,000 hectares of the vineyards of Jerez are the oldest in the world. It is said that the Phoenicians planted vines in about 1000 BC in this area which with 295 days of sunshine every year and a chalky marl soil offers ideal climatic and geological conditions. The method of processing is also ideal for the production of sherry. In the first place, the grapes are not processed mechanically, but trodden out for hours on end by men wearing leather boots. The must is then left to ferment for a year during which time it attains an alcohol percentage of 11.5 to 13.5. The rules governing the making of wine by treading are observed. The vats are ventilated; they are only filled threequarters full then opened so that the wine, which is covered by a thick protective crust of yeast known as 'flor', can breathe but does not spoil. The quality of the sherry depends on the flor. Sherries are distinguished in types such as, for example, fino (dry and fragrant with one of the lowest alcohol percentages) and oloroso (strong tasting and with a high percentage of alcohol – this type is usually drunk as an aperitif). Another oddity which would send shivers down the spine of the humblest French winemaker is the system of piling the casks, piped together, in the form of a pyramid. The sherry is always tapped from the bottom casks and the young wine poured into the top casks. This explains why sherry never has an age! At Domecq, one of the most important sherry producers with 60 hectares of vineyards, there are casks which have been piled in this way for 300 years.

## JEREZ

While the French have never been sherry enthusiasts, the English are extremely fond of it. The English alone consume more than one third of the annual production of approximately a million hectolitres and the greatest brands bear English names – Osborne, John Harvey and Sons, Sandeman, for example. Furthermore, most houses own a bodega in the city where the different types can be tasted. Every year at the begin-

capital, one can see the horses being trained or watch the great parade during the Feria del Caballo held in April, immediately after the Feria of Sevilla.

Who utters the word 'Feria', speaks of Andalusian beauties and flamenco. Here, too, the authentic character has been somewhat lost, but it still remains a marvellous spectacle. The real Andalusian atmosphere, in contrast, can still be found to the full at the Alcázar where every Sunday

ning of September huge harvest festivals are held so that the new wines can be tasted – a truly popular fete. The aristocratic families also devote themselves to a less pedestrian pastime – the breeding of outstanding thoroughbreds, naturally with a great deal of Arab blood in them, which are broken in at the equestrian riding school. This is based on the Spanish Riding School in Vienna. Just as in the Austrian

morning there is a flea market when the local orchestra plays waltzes, paso dobles and marches at a furious tempo.

*Opposite page and above: collegiate church.*
*Top: celebration of the grape harvest.*

## GIBRALTAR

For those who still have doubts, Gibraltar provides evidence that Winston Churchill was superstitious. It is popular belief that the British will remain lords and masters of the famous Rock of Gibraltar as long as the Barbary apes – brought here by the Arabs in the 11th century – live there. Churchill gave orders that the number of apes must never fall below thirty five. And so the army watches over the health of the animals, which are the only wild apes in Europe (and conscientiously fed by the soldiers, because you never know!). The reason why Churchill attached so much importance to Gibraltar, which has been a possession of the English Crown since 1704, is that this less than seven square kilometre chunk of rock controls the narrowest point (precisely 425 metres) of the en-trance to the Mediterranean Sea. It therefore lies in an extremely favou-rable position and during the last war it was of great service to the allies. To convince oneself of the great strate-gic importance of this point, all one has to do is take the cable lift to the top and in clear weather one can see not only the marvellous landscape but also the coast of Morocco, only 18 kilometres away. The town itself, built on the least steep slope of the rock, is not particularly interesting. At the most one feels a little out of place because one has left Spain and suddenly arrived in England. The main street is known, naturally, as Main Street and at the end of the afternoon the 'natives' sit in the pub. To be honest, tourists visit Gibraltar mainly because it is a free port and petrol, like eveything else, is free of excise duty!

*Opposite page: Gibraltar.*
*This page: top, the sounthernmost*
*point of Spain; above, one of the wild*
*monkeys that are being protected by*
*the British army.*

## WHITE VILLAGES

They are called the 'white villages'. The houses have been whitewashed generation after generation, so that one sometimes wonders if the walls do not consist of pure plaster, and they are the symbol of Andalusia. Under the burning sun or under the threatening clouds, they are always blinding white. When an old woman in black or a man on a donkey, legs dangling free, passes by the light suddenly begins to shimmer and the white seems even more glaring. Most of them have still not been discovered by the tourist masses (although the Ministry of Culture has had the – misbegotten? – idea of listing them and producing a map on which they can all be found) and the inhabitants still honour a tradition of hospitality that the rest of Spain has long abandoned. Here the stranger is still a guest and it is a duty and a pleasure to receive him. But make no mistake, the ancestors of these smiling villagers knew extremely difficult times, because the whole of Andalusia was once the theatre in which the wars between the Christians and Moslems was staged. This explains why so many towns have 'de la Frontera' after their names – after every battle the frontier was shifted yet again, depending on which side had been victorious.

*Above: the village of Alozaina.*
*Opposite page: top, the Triana*
*chapel; bottom, an old Andalusian*
*woman.*
*Following pages: farm in the vicinity*
*of Vallamartin.*

77

## WHITE VILLAGES

In days gone by, people used the slightest elevation in the terrain to build a stronghold. Still today the remains – well preserved or not so well preserved – of such structures stand out above groups of chalk-white houses which can be seen from kilometres off, lying between arrow straight rows of olive trees which seem to stretch out to eternity.

Strangely enough the gypsies, as in Grenada, were happy to live in caves (if one believes the tale in the Manuscript of Zaragoza, the cave complex was a great deal more than simply a shelter). In Guadix one can get some idea of the complexity of such a network of dark houses. Like the villages which surround it, Guadix is spotlessly white and, moreover, it has cave dwellings in which the temperature, summer and winter, is 20°C. If one climbs up to the Alcazaba, built by the Arabs on an artificial hill (for obvious strategic

*Above: Olvera.*

*Right: El Castor.*

*Opposite page: top, troglodytic village; bottom, Arcos de la Frontera.*

*Following pages: the city of Ronda.*

reasons they considered the region to be too flat), one finds a mass of caves, their presence only revealed by the ventilation shafts. Six kilometres further on lies Purullena, which is familiar to many more tourists (probably because very nice earthenware is sold and the chalk rocks in the area provide spectacular photographs) and which also has cave dwellings, most of them excavated by the hand of man.

## RONDA

Nowadays, who does not think of Carmen when they hear the name Ronda – it was here that the 'true' events on which Merimée based his novel took place – or of the goddess Julia Jiménez Johnson, who played the role in Francesco Rossi's opera-film?

The last scenes between Carmen and Don José were actually shot in the marvellous arenas of Ronda. This was not simply because of the majestic decor, of course. Ronda, with its crazy three-arched bridge over the 90-metre deep ravine that seperates the old city (one of oldest in Spain) from the new, is a symbol for lovers of the corrida.

Ronda, with its 120-metre perpendicular cliffs and its pure white houses. Ronda, where the rules for fighting bulls on foot were drawn up (see page 96) and where next to the bull ring (the oldest in Spain) a museum of the corrida has been established in which, besides relics, canvasses by Goya can also be admired.

Ronda is a real eagle's nest and in the past fierce fighting has taken place there at various times. Until 1485 it was in the hands of the Moors, who only surrendered after a 20-day battle with the Christians. The armies of Napoleon came to Ronda in 1808; in the cathedral the evidence of these various 'visits' can be found as if in the pages of a history book.

## MARBELLA

Those who are convinced that Spain attracts only 'ordinary' people should visit Marbella. They will be surprised to discover the chic hotels, the expensive cars, the village that is exquisitely maintained thanks to the fact that the rich guests line the municipal coffers so. People go to the golf course, to the thermal baths, and to the pleasant sqaure with the orange trees which is flooded with tourists. But so what? Isn't that just so typically Spanish?

A few kilometres further on lies Puerto Banus, the spitting image of a chic watersports centre, a cross between Saint-Tropez and Cannes. The Rolls appears to be the most popular form of transport. Here are the women of one's dreams, often on the arm of men more likely to give one nightmares... but so what? The fabulous boats moored here seldom see anything other than the quay, their owners apparently afraid the crew will crease their neatly-pressed

uniforms. In the evenings these beautiful people can be found in nightclubs where the noise is enough to wake the dead. Perhaps they are trying to forget their daily lives which are so indolent that they cannot even summon up the energy to take a dip in the sea so close by. That is too exhausting, or perhaps too bourgoise, an activity, for the guests at this curious place, many of which come from what are so euphemistically called the 'Gulf States'.

Could that indeed be the reason that so many (modern) villas are in an unashamed Moorish style?

## VALENCIA

Valencia can be summed up in a word – the Fallas. A huge festival in the week before March 19th, the day of San José, when the streets are flooded with people. In the 18th century woodworkers were in the habit of lighting huge fires of wood shavings in honour of their patron. It was not long before they began to make caricatural wooden dolls – perhaps to tease a neighbour. The neighbour soon became the authorities and the figures became increasingly bigger and more beautiful (some of them are as much as 15 metres tall!). They developed into works of art and eventually a competition was organized. All week long orchestras play all over the city and people throng into the Palacio de la Lonja where small dolls are exhibited. Flowers are offered to the

*Above and opposite page: pictures of the Fallas at Valencia, a fiesta with dancing, parades, and fireworks, lasting a week.*

Madonna of the basilica, doubtless to apologize for disturbing her peace and quiet with the notorious 'mascletas'. Ten days before the beginning of the festival the best maker of fireworks in the city is allowed to demonstrate his skill; the attentive public is regaled with a concert of thundering cracks, carefully built up to a grand, explosive finale. And woe to the firework maker who does not orchestrate his bangs in the proper manner – he is jeered and booed by the knowledgeable public – not a sound for sensitive ears!

## BARCELONA

Nowadays people visit Barcelona as often for its art galleries as its old Gothic quarter. The city has been wholly captivated by the 'movida' and is enjoying freedom and creativity to the full. The nights in Barcelona are wild, and the days are not bad, either! Gaudi's city has turned to the 'virtues' preached by Almodóver and one sometimes has the impression that the pupil overshadows the master! But with someone like

original commission was offered to the architect Villar, who wanted to build a Neo-Gothic church. His successor, Gaudi, completed the crypt according to Villar's design but then developed his own plans – a gigantic, 150-metre-high presbytery, three facades, twelve spires (one for each apostle), a steeple dedicated to the Virgin Mary and a spire in the centre, dedicated to Christ, rising above all the others and surrounded by four steeples representing the evange-

*Top: the Sagrada Familia de Gaudi; above: the caravel of Christopher Columbus.*
*Opposite page: a statue of Christopher Columbus.*

Mariscal it is indeed difficult to resist the temptation of all that is new, all the more so because the city has produced geniuses such as Pablo Picasso, Joan Miró and Salvador Dalí.

Yet admirers of old buildings can take heart – this does not mean that the Olympic city has renounced its past, and the Sagrada Familia is still unfinished. The story of this temple of penitence is a curious one. The

lists. But in 1926 Gaudi was knocked down by a tram and died before he could complete his masterwork. Building continued, even though it has cost huge amounts of money and endless discussions have taken place regarding the proper interpretation of the drawings left by the master.

## BARCELONA

While Gaudí's edifices caused great controversies, there is one monument – in fact, a whole quarter – about which there is general agreement. This is the Barrio Gótico which contains the cathedral. It took 150 years to build this flawless example of Catalonian Gothic architecture. It is magnificent and at the same time extremely pure in form, a handsome piece of architecture and time should be taken to enjoy the smallest detail such as, for example, the famous centre dome (begun in 1422 and completed in...1913!), the Christus del Lepanto, or the beautiful cloister around the garden with its palm trees and magnolias.

Gaudí's works can be found everywhere in Barcelona, from Parc Güell to the Casa Vicenc, but it is also worth seeing the Roman remains and

*Above: the Güell park.*
*Opposite page: top left, a sculpture by Miro; top right, the towers of the Sagrada Famila; below, the Casa Vicenç.*

Middle Ages edifices such as La Canoja, an 11th century poorhouse, or the Pla Berenguer el Gran with its Gothic houses built on the Roman walls.

Further on one finds the Ramblas, where it is busy from the morning to the evening and from the evening to the morning, and which has resisted many trends. The Ramblas are a sort of cross between the Champs-Elysées and the Boulevard Saint-Michel and have become so symbolic of Barcelona that their function has been forgotten – they form the route to the harbour. For centuries Barcelona has been first and foremost a harbour; a replica of Christopher Columbus's carvel, cradled in the water at the quayside, is a silent witness to this.

Below: the monastery of Santiago de
Compostela and the insignia of the
town.
Opposite page: the statue of Santiago
de Compostela.

## SANTIAGO DE COMPOSTELA

According to legend the body of
Saint Jacobus, who died a martyr's
death in Jerusalem in 44 AD, was
brought to Spain by his disciples. At
the beginning of the 9th century a
farmer, guided by a mysterious light,
rediscovered his remains. This was
the start of the Reconquista; at the
time the Christians had somewhat
lost heart for the struggle against the
Moors, but after this discovery they
joined battle as one man, though it is
extremely doubtful whether Saint
Jacobus actually found himself on –
or in – Spanish soil. But no matter,
inspired by the appearance of the
'white knight', the soldiers per-
formed many heroic deeds. Succes-
sive kings ensured that a shrine was
built for the relics of the apostle who
was the driving force behind the holy
struggle. When Al Mansour razed
the city to the ground (but spared the
grave), Alfonso VI commissioned a
cathedral to be built on the site of the
old church and this quickly became
an important place of pilgrimage. So
great was the interest in Saint Jacobus that Pope Calixtus II ruled that a
year in which his feast day fell on a
Sunday would be proclaimed a holy
year. A large number of pilgrims still
come to the cathedral, which has
four courtyards, in order to climb the
steps to the high altar to the richly
adorned 13th-century statue of Saint
Jacobus and kiss the hem of his
cloak. But a sojourn in the Hostal de
los Reyes Católicos, founded by
Ferdinand and Isabella, is a lot more
comfortable today than it was in the
days of great pilgrimages because
the guesthouse has now become an
extremely chic 'parador'.

## THE BEACHES AND HARBOURS OF GALICIA

The Romans named one of the capes Finis Terrae and in so doing characterized the whole province which borders the Atlantic Ocean and which is enclosed by mountain ranges to the north and east. It is so isolated that the Moors barely visited it. Galicia has the fact that half its territory lies between 400 and 600 metres above sea level to thank for its soft, wet climate. Precipitation is more than a metre per year, which the Galicians generally accept with humour; they say that in Santiago de Compostela rain is an art form. Galicians do not like big cities; the majority of them live in small villages and they are so attached to their land that until now every attempt at land redistribution has failed. Understandable, because most plots lie on slo-ping ground and are therefore unsuitable for mechanized farming and, furthermore, the little green patches of land give the landscape its charm. Beach and nature lovers know this all too well; they go off in search of peaceful coves half hidden along the shores of the rías, bays where the tide flows freely. Of course, the purists think it a pity that the little island of Islas Cíes has been linked to the mainland by a 2-kilometre long bridge. But the inhabitants have resolved to safeguard their own identity and would rather play the gaita, a form of bagpipes, than play with concrete.

*Above: Cape Finisterre, the westernmost point of Spain. Opposite page: fishing nets being repaired.*

*Above and right: corrida scenes in
the plaza de toros of Sevilla.
Opposite page: the Plaza de Toros in
Jerez.*

## THE CORRIDA

The bullfight has both impassioned admirers and obdurate opponents. Bullfighting has been raised to an art form and every year attracts large numbers of aficionados to the arenas where they fight for the best, and most expensive, places. The corrida has its heroes – men and bulls – and its martyrs; matadors impaled on the horns of a bull, dying within minutes, their femoral artery ripped open. The fight appears unequal, but is no less dangerous for that; a great number of matadors have paid for their audacity with their lives.

Bullfighting was once the sport of the aristocracy – it is said that El Cid celebrated his victory by fighting a bull – but Philip V of Anjou forbad the nobility from taking part, for fear that his court would be needlessly depleted! And so the corrida became a popular people's pastime. The first professional bullfighter was a carpenter from Ronda. His son, Pedro Romero, who lived at the end of the 18th century and who is regarded as the father of the bullfight, killed 5,500 bulls according to the stories.

A corrida is an exceptionally intense spectacle, in which the virtuosity of the matador makes one almost forget the fatal outcome. Every gesture and every pass has a name and for the torero the art is to make as many different movements – veronicas, chicuelinas, gaoneras, etc. – with his cape as possible in order to place the bull where he wants it and how he wants it. An exceptionally courageous bull arouses the enthusiasm of the public, who wave cushions to demand that its life be spared.

## SPAIN AS AN AGRICULTURAL DOMAIN

Oranges from Valencia, asparagus and strawberries from Aranjuez, cheese from La Mancha, jamón serrano and almonds from Andalusia – whether the soil is fertile or barren, whether there is too much rain or too little, Spanish farmers have always managed to achieve miracles with the land God has given them. Spain comes just after Italy as Europe's second largest producer of fruit, and produces a great deal more than it consumes itself. With 5% of total world production, it is the world's third largest orange grower, while more than 10% of the world's lemons and approximately 15% of its mandarines come from Spain.

In contrast, grain yields and even wine production are fairly small. This is because the soil is still worked in the old traditional manner due to lack of financial resources. Moreover, farms are still fairly small

*Above: oranges being sold.*
*Right: flowering almond-trees.*
*Opposite page: top, the Sierra Nevada; bottom, orange-trees.*

*Following pages: almond-tree landscape.*

98

and have to support a large number of people. It is the very things which give this tranquil country its charm which are the obstacles to modern management. Specially for the economists let us take the example of Andalusia, where more than 20% of the population work in agriculture. This is far too high a percentage, any child knows that! Threequarters of these are day labourers; that is to say they do not own any land and 'hire' themselves out by the day. Every summer some twenty thousand agricultural labourers trek to France, where they have to compete fiercely with mechanization, to offer their services. For reasons already mentioned, meat production in Spain is lower than that in France, though Spain has a lot more sheep and pigs.

## MALLORCA

The Balearics, so famous for their beaches, have become the cheapest and closest sunny destination for North Europeans. The result of this is that in the high season the beauty of these islands disappears under a flood of tourists. But Palma, the capital of Mallorca, seems little changed since Chopin and George Sand came to enjoy their secret love. Here one always walks "among the palms, the cedars, the aloes, the orange, lemon, fig and pomegranate trees. The skies are turquoise, the sea blue, the hills emerald green. And the light? The light is just as blue as the skies, the sun shines all day long", wrote an enchanted Chopin. But one also walks among concrete, some of it so horrendous that after the obligatory visit to places of interest the visitor is well advised to take

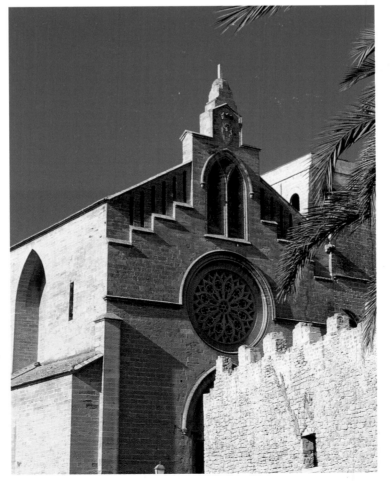

*Above: Palma de Mallorca.*
*Right: church in Alcudia.*
*Opposite page: the palace of*
*Almudaina.*

flight to the beach between Puerto de Andraitx and Purto de Sóller, which is one of the loveliest in the Mediterranean.

But do not forget the wrought-iron canopy that Gaudí designed for the royal box in the cathedral, the Almudaina palace (an old Arab fortress). Take a stroll across the Plaza Mayor and through the streets of the old city where lovely palaces with staircases hidden behind lattice-work and inner courtyards full of flowers can be discovered.

Moreover, on the way out of the city it is certainly well worthwhile stopping at the Castell del Bellver. This severe citadel, completely round, surmounted by a donjon and flanked by three towers, was built in the 14th century for Jaime II.

## MALLORCA

The visitor is advised to get out of the city, and as quickly as possible, to search for the mountain villages the tourists ignore and from which winding paths descend to the turquoise waters of magical coves. To the beach, where all the aromas of the Mediterranean come together. You can watch the fishermen returning as evening falls, when the sea is as smooth as a mirror, barely rippled by the passage of the boats and fect on creativity, for Chopin composed his most beautiful preludes here and countless painters and artists have settled here.

If you enjoy the contrast between nature in all its grandure and rural simplicity this tranquil island offers, you will do well to take the coast road between Andraitx and Sóller which winds between olive trees, orange trees and cultivated terraces and alongside deep clefts at the bottom of which the intense blue sea

glowing in the light of the setting sun. Onwards, ever onwards, to a high cliff where you can dream in the shadow of a collapsed atalaya (a watchtower), of which there are so many along the coast and from which in the 16th century the people defended themselves against the Moslem pirates, just as the romantics, who could never get enough of the sea, dreamed. The climate of Mallorca must have a favourable ef-

glitters. Along this route one comes across names such as Estellenchs, La Granja, Valldemosa (where one can visit the rooms where Chopin and George Sand lived, Deyá and Castell d'Alaro, where one can stop and take a dip in the warm waters of a deserted little bay.

*Top: a creek with turqouise-coloured water.*
*Above and right: Formentera beaches.*
*Opposite page: olive and almond trees.*

## IBIZA

Spain goes crazy on Ibiza. After wild nights in nightclubs famous throughout the world, people spend the days sunbathing on one of the nudist beaches. Clothing is a mixture of hippy, grunge and... in short, anything goes! And that does not only apply to clothing; Ibiza has been regarded as a homosexual paradise for years. Perhaps not a place for those who want a peaceful holiday! Nonetheless, on the northern side of the island (round Punta Grosa), there are still almost deserted coves to discover, visited only by owners of 'sigaren', enormous motorboats with sharp keels which cut through the waves at unbelievable speeds.

To their delight, early risers will discover that they have the town to themselves. Sleeping half the day away has been raised to an art form on Ibiza and it is practised with great devotion. Until at least half past ten the winding streets of the upper town

*Above: Cala Torida.*

*Right: salinas.*

*Opposite page: top, a windmill;*

*bottom, the harbour of Ibiza.*

are deserted and can be enjoyed in peace and quiet, as can the old city walls and the cathedral which has a terrace offering a wonderful view of the harbour.

The museum of modern art does not attract hoards of art lovers but the hotel El Corsario, without doubt the best-known hotel on the island, is a must, even if only for a cup of coffee. This house, one of the oldest on Ibiza, was beautifully restored and rebuilt by an enormously wealthy young German (who turned her back on her aristocratic family and installed herself on the island) and provided the backdrop for Barbet Schroeder's famous film 'More'. Polanski was also inspired by the many patios and staircases, which sometimes appear to lead to nowhere, and shot a few scenes here for his film 'Pirate'.

# CONTENTS

# INDEX

# PHOTO CREDITS